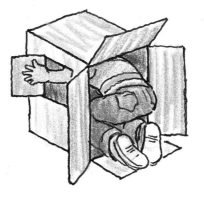
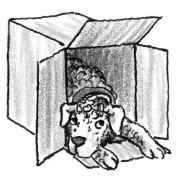

Once there was a HOUSE

Structures devised by
GREGG REYES

Text by
JUDY HINDLEY

Pictures by
ROBERT BARTELT

COLLINS

For children everywhere

William Collins Sons & Co Ltd
London · Glasgow · Sydney · Auckland
Toronto · Johannesburg

First published 1986
© text Gregg Reyes and Judy Hindley 1986
© illustrations Robert Bartelt 1986
ISBN 0 00 195626 4

Printed and bound in Belgium
by Henri Proost & CIE PVBA

Once upon a time . . .

there was a . . . house!

It was a good house.
It was small. It was safe. It was cosy.

This house
could go

anywhere you wanted.

But when you got there
you couldn't see outside.

Once there was a house
with a window.

You could see people.
They could see you.
But . . .
you could not go
in and out.

Bother!

Once there was a house
with a door
and a roof
and a chimney
and an aerial
and gutters
and pipes
to drain the rain away –
and shutters
and a flower box
and a dog kennel –
Wow!

The postman could put letters through the letter box.

The milkman could put bottles in the crates.

The dustman could take away the rubbish.

But, oh – what a shame – there were no other houses in the street.

Once upon a time
there was another house.
This house had furniture.
It had a cooker and a table
and a sink.
In this house there was a lot to do.
Wash the dishes! Bake the cakes!
Do the shopping!

Once there was a very busy street.
It had houses and a crossing
and a petrol station!
Fill the tank! Check the oil!
Wash the windows! Change the tyres!
What a house!
What a petrol station!
What a busy street!

21

And all of it was made
by you and me.

HOW THE HOUSE WAS MADE

A large, strong box is one of the best toys in the world. It can become a train, an aeroplane, a car, a house – or whatever a child's imagination stretches to. The biggest boxes come from TV rental shops and shops that sell large domestic appliances. They are well worth hunting for. Some are big enough for a couple of toddlers to stand inside.

Even the heaviest cardboard is easy to handle if you score it and brush it with water. *To score*, make a deep scratch to weaken the cardboard in the place where you want to bend or cut it. You can use a knife or a scissors-point, guiding it with a ruler. (You can also make an excellent saw from the cutting edge of a cling film dispenser. Just peel it off and reinforce it with a strip of heavy card.)

To cut without scissors, score a deep scratch and then brush water over it to weaken it. (Use a little water-colour brush.) You can soften it enough this way for a child to 'cut' it with a ruler, or make a neat clean hole in it with a finger or a pencil.

And remember, cardboard burns easily so it should never come near a flame.

To make the basic house

Set the box on end to leave a strong base at the bottom (this is important). When you cut out the door, leave a small ledge. Score the hinge side and fold the door back sharply against something with a hard edge, like a ruler. Fold the front and back flaps into triangles and attach the sides with toggles. For each toggle, make two holes in each of the roof flaps.

Finish the roof by covering it completely with another piece of cardboard, cut to size.

Fold into triangles

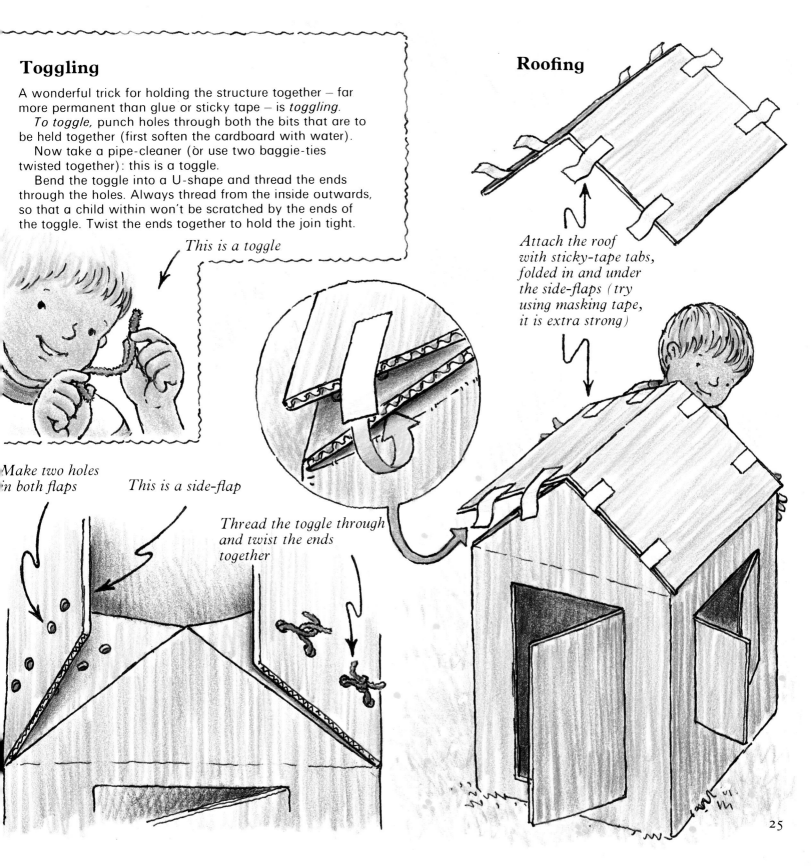

Toggling

A wonderful trick for holding the structure together – far more permanent than glue or sticky tape – is *toggling*.

To toggle, punch holes through both the bits that are to be held together (first soften the cardboard with water).

Now take a pipe-cleaner (òr use two baggie-ties twisted together): this is a toggle.

Bend the toggle into a U-shape and thread the ends through the holes. Always thread from the inside outwards, so that a child within won't be scratched by the ends of the toggle. Twist the ends together to hold the join tight.

This is a toggle

Make two holes in both flaps

This is a side-flap

Thread the toggle through and twist the ends together

Roofing

Attach the roof with sticky-tape tabs, folded in and under the side-flaps (try using masking tape, it is extra strong)

25

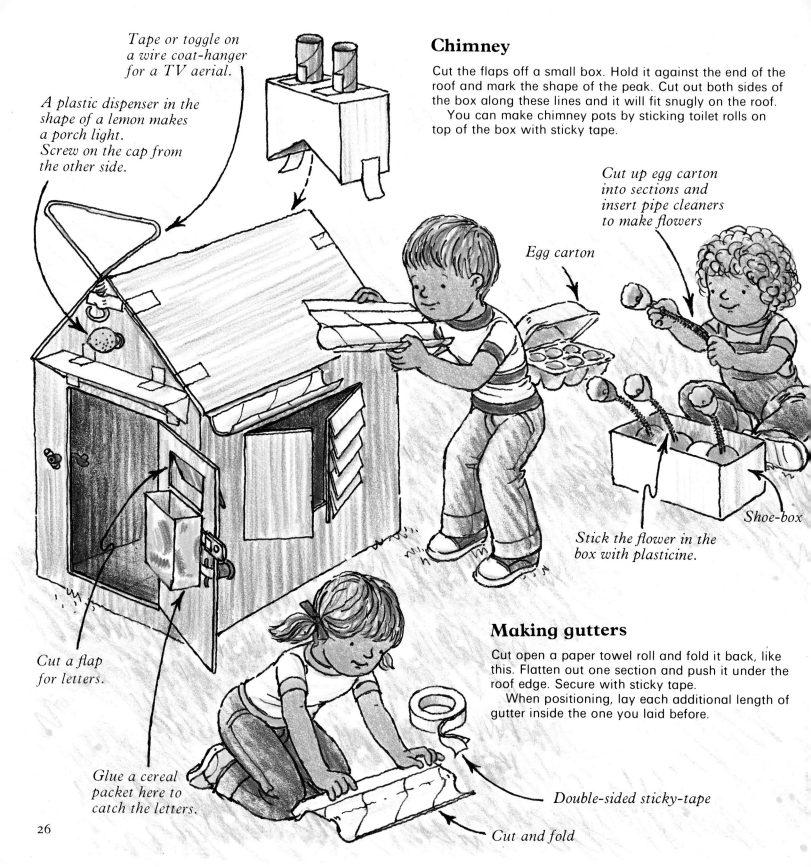

Tape or toggle on a wire coat-hanger for a TV aerial.

A plastic dispenser in the shape of a lemon makes a porch light. Screw on the cap from the other side.

Chimney

Cut the flaps off a small box. Hold it against the end of the roof and mark the shape of the peak. Cut out both sides of the box along these lines and it will fit snugly on the roof.

You can make chimney pots by sticking toilet rolls on top of the box with sticky tape.

Cut up egg carton into sections and insert pipe cleaners to make flowers

Egg carton

Cut a flap for letters.

Stick the flower in the box with plasticine.

Shoe-box

Making gutters

Cut open a paper towel roll and fold it back, like this. Flatten out one section and push it under the roof edge. Secure with sticky tape.

When positioning, lay each additional length of gutter inside the one you laid before.

Glue a cereal packet here to catch the letters.

Double-sided sticky-tape

Cut and fold

Shutters

To make shutters, cut two flaps and fold them back like this. (Remember to score and brush with water, to cut more easily.)

For louvres, cut strips of cardboard slightly less wide than the shutter, using one strip as a pattern for all the rest. Stick two strips of double-sided tape down each shutter. Lay the 'louvres' on it from bottom to top, so that they overlap as they go up.

Curtains

For each curtain, cut a strip of double-sided sticky tape about one third the width of the window. Fold a paper cloth into little pleats along the exposed side of the tape.

Then strip the backing from the tape and stick it just above the window, inside the house. (To do this, you will probably have to crawl inside.)

Door knob and lock

For a door knob, toggle a cotton-reel to the door, like this.

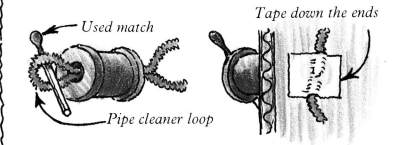

Used match

Tape down the ends

Pipe cleaner loop

It's particularly magical to have a door that can be 'locked' from within, so that the child inside can feel quite private.

For a 'locking' mechanism, pull off the top of an empty washing-up liquid dispenser (it comes off easily). Make a hole in the doorframe big enough for the lower part of the 'lock' to fit through.

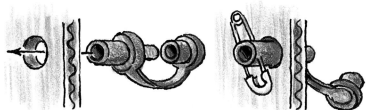

Push it through, holding it in place with a safety pin. (The plastic can be easily pierced by a pin.)

The 'latch' is a strip of cardboard. Make a hole just at the end, so that it fits over the dispenser nozzle. Then tape the latch into position on the door.

When the cap is put on the nozzle, it locks the latch in place.

It might be a good idea to practise this mechanism first on a door cut into a small box — otherwise you may have to demonstrate by reaching in through the window!

HOW THE FURNITURE WAS MADE

The chest has drawers that slide in and out and the sink
has running water . . . the only trick is finding the right
materials. Remember that cardboard cuts like butter if you
prepare it properly. Be sure to score and brush thoroughly
with water along the line you want to cut.

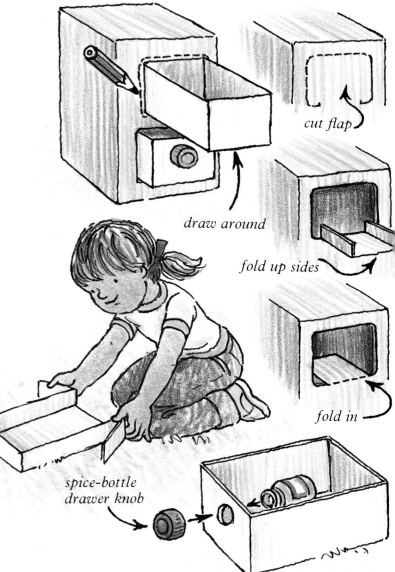

cut flap

draw around

fold up sides

fold in

To make the chest of drawers you need a
couple of shoe-boxes for drawers and a larger box to fit
them into. The lids of the shoe-boxes are used to
strengthen the shelves.

1 Hold each shoe-box in turn against the side of the
   larger box and mark where the drawers go.
2 Cut along the line as shown to make a flap.
3 Bend in the sides . . .
   and fold in the flap to make a shelf.
4 Cut away one end of the rim of the shoe-box lid to make
   two tabs, as shown. Glue the lid down onto the shelf,
   gluing the tabs just inside the box on either side of the
   opening.

To make a knob for the drawer, screw together the two
parts of a very small screw-top jar (try an empty spice-
bottle) from either side.

*spice-bottle
drawer knob*

*reach from underneath
to screw on the tap.*

To make the sink you need (as well as a small,
strong box) a waterproof container, such as a large ice-
cream container or a plastic storage box, with a rim
around the edge. For the tap, you need a screw-top
dispenser with a spout that squirts when you depress the
top – a hand-lotion or liquid soap dispenser, for example.
  Push down the 'sink' into a hole in the top of the box,
with its rim just resting on the edge. Make a small hole for
the spout of the 'tap', close enough so that it will squirt
into the sink. Screw together the two parts of the
dispensing bottle through this hole, after filling the bottle
with water.

To make the cooker

Take a sturdy little box and follow the diagrams below to make a super-realistic-looking cooker. Make 'burners' from aluminium pie-plates, dropped into holes cut into the box. Or peel off the covering layer from a piece of cardboard to show the furrowed inner layer. Cut out saucer-sized discs to look like the surfaces of electric burners, and paint them black, or colour them with magic marker. Stick onto cooker top.

The scales

are just pretend ones. Stick together an upturned box lid, a toilet roll tube, and a little box. Use plasticine.

The lamp

is a lemon 'light bulb' stuck into the top of a bottle. The lampshade is made from a piece of folded card secured to a cardboard support.

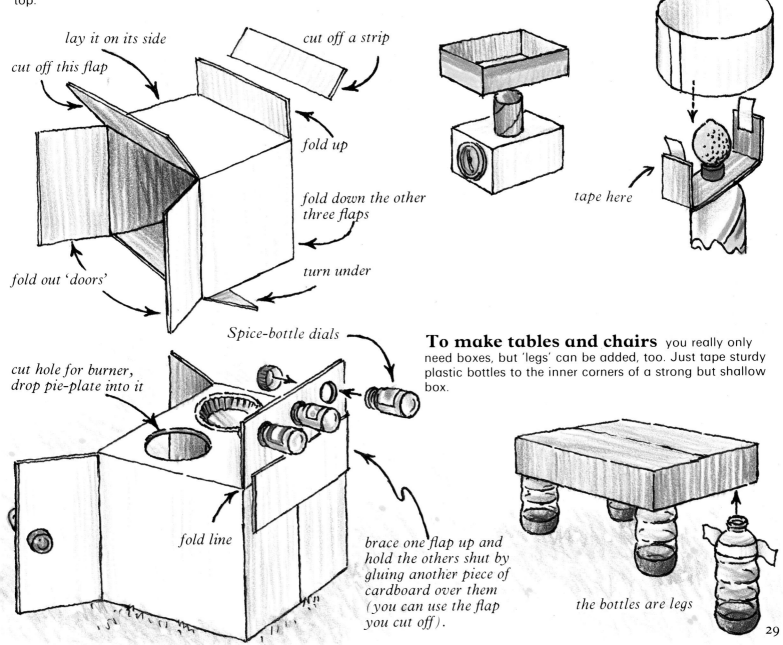

lay it on its side

cut off this flap

cut off a strip

fold up

fold down the other three flaps

fold out 'doors'

turn under

Spice-bottle dials

cut hole for burner, drop pie-plate into it

fold line

brace one flap up and hold the others shut by gluing another piece of cardboard over them (you can use the flap you cut off).

tape here

To make tables and chairs

you really only need boxes, but 'legs' can be added, too. Just tape sturdy plastic bottles to the inner corners of a strong but shallow box.

the bottles are legs

... AND THE CAR AND PETROL STATION

Large structures like this petrol station can be made by cutting and combining the same basic material – cardboard boxes. Don't forget to score the cardboard and soften it with water to make it easier to cut. Remember that if you can't find a box just the size you want, you can cut down another one and extend it, or cut it in two and re-combine the halves.

The tall pillars are made in a variety of ways. One is a long, heavy carpet tube. One is a shorter tube stuck in a tall box packed with wadded newspaper. Others are made by using kitchen roll tubes to hold together a series of rolled-up Sunday newspaper magazines. With this method a tube can be extended as far as you wish.

To make the car, just make an H-shaped cut in a big box (preferably oblong) and bend the resulting flaps as shown.

The petrol pump is just a stack of boxes – it's the proportions that make it look realistic, plus the labelling and the 'gun' made from an empty plastic bottle which hangs from the side of the pump and has a string hose.

Cut lengthwise

Attach with thick string

Cut out this shape

Fold down

Fold up

Paint on wheels

Cut out a flap for the 'bonnet'

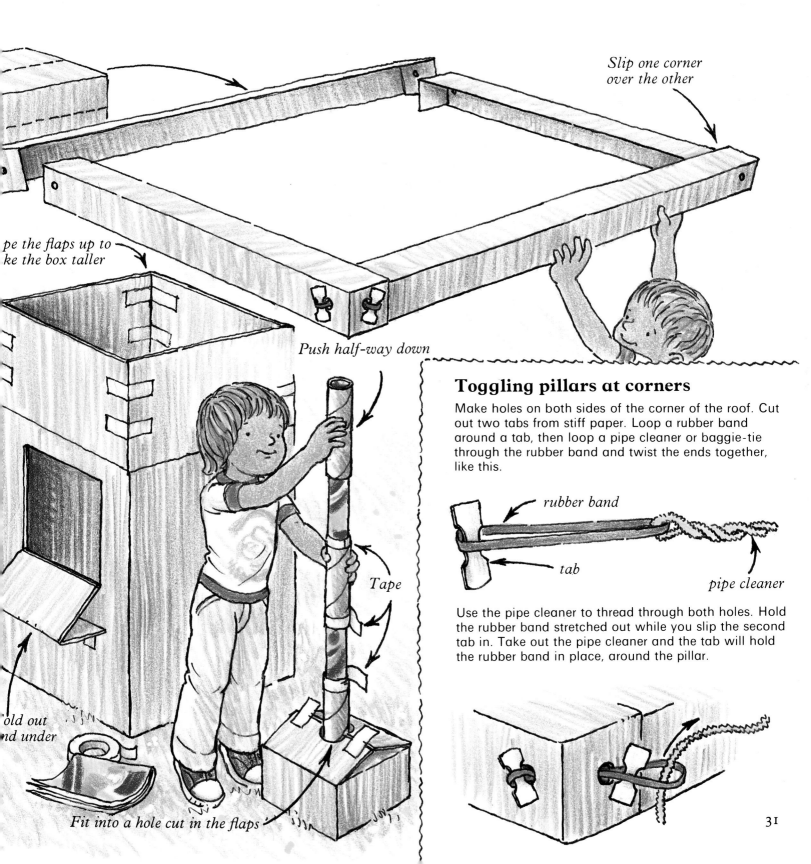

Slip one corner
over the other

pe the flaps up to
ke the box taller

Push half-way down

old out
nd under

Tape

Fit into a hole cut in the flaps

Toggling pillars at corners

Make holes on both sides of the corner of the roof. Cut out two tabs from stiff paper. Loop a rubber band around a tab, then loop a pipe cleaner or baggie-tie through the rubber band and twist the ends together, like this.

rubber band

tab

pipe cleaner

Use the pipe cleaner to thread through both holes. Hold the rubber band stretched out while you slip the second tab in. Take out the pipe cleaner and the tab will hold the rubber band in place, around the pillar.

31

... AND TOOLS AND THINGS

'Tools' can be astonishingly simple. A shampoo bottle with a long neck, taped to a rolled-up magazine, readily becomes a hammer. Pipe-cleaners are flux (soldering sticks) — you 'melt' them with your blow torch to repair your car. A small box with a window is a welding helmet.

Notice the magical effect of paint and lettering, signs and labels. A box with a familiar, brilliant symbol becomes a petrol pump. A pipe cleaner pushed through the centre of the lid of a margerine tub marked with numerals turns it into a gauge (or a clock face).

Keep going and have fun!

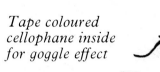

Tape coloured cellophane inside for goggle effect

Cut out the sides

Pliers

Tape ice-lolly sticks to clothes-peg

Hammer

Tape like this

Battery and recharger

A row of washing-up liquid bottle tops makes a battery recharger (two rows makes a battery). Two clothes-pegs and some string complete it.

Re-label two washing-up liquid bottles. Remove tops and thread string through each top. Tie a large knot at the end of each piece of string to retain it, then replace the tops. Now thread the other two ends through another bottle top dispenser, and secure with tape.

Air gauges and clock

Tub lid fixed with pipe cleaner and tab

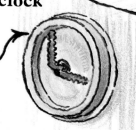